Life in a
Tudor
Palace

Life in a

Tudor

Palace

THE SUTTON LIFE SERIES

Life in a
Tudor
Palace

Christopher Gidlow

SUTTON PUBLISHING

Sutton Publishing Limited
Phoenix Mill · Thrupp · Stroud
Gloucestershire · GL5 2BU

First published 2007

British Library Cataloguing in Publication Data
A catalogue for this book is available from the British Library.

ISBN: 978-0-7509-4608-7

Typeset in Bembo.
Typesetting and origination by
Sutton Publishing Limited.
Printed and bound in England.

Contents

CHAPTER 1

Introduction

The reign of King Henry VIII was one of the great dramas of English history. As often as not this drama was played out on the magnificent stage provided by his palaces.

By inheritance, confiscation and construction, King Henry amassed some sixty residences, of which two-thirds were in regular use. They ranged from ancient castles (Windsor and the Tower of London), rambling hunting lodges (Woodstock) and glorified manor houses (Eltham), to newly constructed Tudor palaces such as those at Nonsuch, Hampton Court and Whitehall.

Among these many residences seven stood out, the so-called 'Great Houses', at Greenwich, Westminster/

Whitehall, Hampton Court, Woodstock, Richmond, Eltham and Beaulieu. It is on life in these Tudor palaces that this book focuses.

These palaces were symbols of Henry VIII's power and magnificence, and also practical bases from which he could govern the kingdom while enjoying his favourite pastimes. They were residences, too, of the extensive Tudor Court. The court existed to serve the king, from the 'gong-scourers' who cleaned out the toilets, to the Lord Great Master, one of the highest nobles in the land.

The palaces of Tudor England have all but vanished, victims of accidental fires or changes in taste. The Great Halls of Eltham and Westminster, already old in Henry's time, still stand, if in much altered surroundings. Only at Hampton Court do substantial remnants of the main apartments, courtiers' lodgings and the kitchens that served them survive to be visited. Even here, the private chambers of the king and his family have vanished.

For evidence, we must search the account books, which record the vast expenditure lavished on the buildings and the food and wages of those who worked within. Detailed inventories of the palaces taken on Henry's death offer tantalising glimpses of the mundane and the magnificent objects that filled them. Additionally, ambassadors and courtiers themselves left accounts, which illuminate life within the walls.

We have one very significant piece of information on how a Tudor palace functioned. In 1527, King Henry VIII and his Council (which in practice meant his all-powerful Lord Chancellor, Cardinal Thomas Wolsey) issued the Eltham Ordinances. These were detailed rules for 'the establishment of good order and reformation of sundry errors and misuses' in the court.

The Ordinances, in a bound volume, signed by the king, were kept in the Compting House, the office of the palace accountants. Here they could be consulted regularly by the head officers of the chamber and household. The councillors would make quarterly inspections of the palaces to ensure the Ordinances were being kept.

These Ordinances provide an invaluable record of how the meticulously minded cardinal wanted the court to function, with the minimum of mistakes and un-necessary waste. In reality, the court was dynamic and fluid, dominated by the changing whims of the larger-than-life monarch and the personalities who surrounded him. The great cardinal himself lost power barely two years after the Ordinances were drawn up. We can see in them, however, both the theory he had tried to impose and the problems that could arise to challenge it.

We shall follow King Henry VIII and his court through a typical day at a Tudor palace, between the publication of the Ordinances at Eltham Palace in 1527 and his death at Westminster/Whitehall Palace in 1547. In practice there was no such thing as a 'typical' day over that period, which encompassed six wives, the fall and execution of numerous ministers, a split with Rome and the physical degeneration of an ageing, ailing monarch. We shall imagine, though, a day that was not a particular feast day, one without any specific great business to attend to or important visitors to be received; a very ordinary day, of which most of the history of the time must have been composed.

CHAPTER 2

The Tudor Court

The way a Tudor palace worked derived from the much simpler pattern of noble life in the Middle Ages. The main building used by a medieval noble was the Great Hall. This was used for public life, eating and as a place where servants could sleep. At the back of the hall would be a separate room, a chamber, in which the lord would sleep, conduct private business and be entertained. At the opposite end you would find separate kitchens, stables and stores.

The hall and its dependencies were the responsibility of the Steward, while the chamber was the domain of the Chamberlain.

This traditional structure continued, in a magnified and more complex form, in the Tudor palaces. Here, the Lord

Steward presided over the household, the Great Hall and the departments necessary to its functioning, while the Lord Chamberlain looked after the 'chamber', aspects of the king's private life as well as his actual bedroom.

The buildings where the court resided were largely incidental. The structure remained the same, whatever its physical surroundings. The king travelled from residence to residence. His favourite palace was Greenwich. Business kept him at Westminster or the neighbouring Whitehall for much of the year, and Windsor Castle was his principal residence outside London. Next in favour came the newly built Hampton Court Palace.

The court arrives

The Tudor palaces were massive complexes, which dominated their surrounding areas. Towers, pinnacles, chimneys and vanes signalled their presence from afar.

The first warning that the king was on his way would be the harbingers galloping into view. Led by the knight harbinger, these men were responsible for preparing the king's arrival and assigning lodgings for the courtiers who accompanied him. Shortly afterwards, the gentle-men ushers and yeoman ushers would arrive.

The harbingers and ushers had with them a book, signed by the king, 'describing the number of every person, of what estate, degree or condition he be' who was allowed to lodge in or around the palace. They were ordered, on pain of losing their offices, not to give lodgings to anyone else unless directed by the king or council. If there were more courtiers than the palace could accommodate, local householders might be compelled to offer hospitality. The ushers would take note of what items were left in the lodging and take charge of the keys. Householders were paid double compensation for any losses caused by thoughtless young nobles making free with their property.

The palaces had 'abiding households' that looked after them while the king was elsewhere. Although it was possible for the court to arrive unexpectedly, in practice its movements were fairly regular. The king tended to stay in Whitehall for the law terms, when Parliament sat. Itineraries were worked out in advance, with the court moving every few weeks in summer. In the winter, it might move even more frequently, except when hindered by the weather. Even the best plans could be thrown into disarray by an outbreak of plague, forcing it to move swiftly to a more healthy location.

A Tudor would not have wondered why the court moved. This had been the regular custom for as long as there had been kings. One reason was the demand the court placed on its location, devouring food stocks, over-hunting the parks and monopolising lodgings. Another was for the king to display himself to his subjects. Although moving the court was difficult, it was easier for the king to move to meet his people than for them to travel to see him. We can also imagine that a change of scene simply added to the king's enjoyment of life, preventing him from getting too bored.

An important early arrival was the clerk of the market. He would note local economic conditions, then set 'convenient and reasonable' prices for food and drink, fodder, lodging and bedding. He would check local weights and measures and source seasonally good and wholesome provisions. This was an important safeguard, since otherwise prices would be bound to rise with the arrival of so many wealthy consumers.

Soon the road leading to the palace would be creaking with the carts of the Lord Steward's men. The offices, as the different departments were called, had their own staff and equipment carts. Their job was to set up the kitchens so that there would be food waiting when the rest of the court arrived.

There was always work to be done to make the palace ready. Carpenters, joiners, masons, painters and other craftsmen worked swiftly, going from chamber to chamber. The accommodation would be swept, washed and dusted. Unforeseen circumstances gave rise to extra work. For example, before the first arrival of Queen Anne Boleyn at Hampton Court, craftsmen laboured through the night removing all references to Catherine of Aragon. Three years later they had to repeat the process, replacing Anne's decorations with ones relating to Jane Seymour!

Yeomen and grooms of the Wardrobe hung the chambers and set the soft furnishings, including the beds. The 'Standing Wardrobes' were large stores, for beds, arrases (large Flemish tapestries), great carpets, cushions and hangings, and ladders to put them up. The Wardrobe of the Robes was used for clothes and the Jewel House for the king's small personal items.

The palace and surrounding area were designated as 'the Verge'. Within the Verge, law and order were kept by the knight marshall and his officers and deputies, with cases heard by the Lord Steward or his under-steward. This saved wrangling with local sheriffs and mayors, and reflected the seriousness of crimes committed close to the king. Assaults on courtiers within the Verge were punishable by loss of the offending hand. It was under-stood, however, that beating errant servants, even to the extent of drawing blood, was perfectly permissible.

The knight marshall and his officers excluded 'boys and vile persons', punished vagabonds and 'mighty beggars' and took 'good regard' of the 'unthrifty and common women' who followed the court. As occasion demanded, these would be banished from the palace and its vicinity.

Most of the palaces stood on the Thames, which meant that the court would often arrive by water.

The king's main entrance was the watergate, connected by a gallery directly to his chambers. Other courtiers and staff would pass through the distinctive Gate House. To facilitate travel by boat, the astronomical clock at Hampton Court gave the time of the tides. Alternatively, the king might come by road from one of his lesser houses. However he arrived, he expected to find a newly decorated and clean palace, with the Lord Steward standing at the entrance ready to present him with the keys.

The people of the palace

Once the whole court had arrived, there would be about 800 men, 200 of whom were part of the Lord Steward's department, not including guests or those serving the queen or the royal children. With up to 1,000 inhabitants, a Tudor palace would have a population equivalent to a small market town.

Almost all those who worked at the palace were men. Women were put on the payroll for low-paid seasonal work, such as weeding. The king contracted a fine laundress, Anne Harris, to wash his own linen. There were also women with specialist accomplishments such as musicians or Levinia Teerlinc, a portrait painter. One 'wife who makes the king's puddings' worked among the men in the kitchens at Hampton Court.

The queen also had women to attend her, close companions such as her ladies-in-waiting, but her staff members were generally men. Catherine of Aragon had a household of 200. Catherine Parr, who lived more simply than Henry's previous wives, still had a household of seventy and a chamber of thirty-nine. The king's son had his wet-nurse and, once weaned, a dry-nurse; but, like his father, he was attended by men.

The people of the palaces were generally young, though it is difficult to pin down their exact ages: the pages would probably have been young teenagers, but the 'boys' who turned the spits in the Great Kitchen were probably strapping young adults. A large number of the courtiers would have been under 21. Many others were in their twenties.

For much of his reign, Henry VIII would have been one of the oldest people at court. He liked to be surrounded by active young people, which increased his feeling of virility. Apart from Catherine of Aragon, all his wives were younger, often considerably younger, than himself, which added to the youthful atmosphere of the palace.

Tudor society was hierarchical, with the king at the top. The court was the main way of advancing in society. It was important to attract the notice of the king and gain his favour, so courtiers would continually try to get close to the king. In return, the king depended on courtiers to govern the country.

A person's position in the hierarchy determined where he or she worked, ate, slept and even went to the toilet in the palace. Most inhabitants of Tudor England ranked simply as 'men and wives'. They had no land and worked for other people. Above them came the yeomen, small-holders with their own land, and masters and mistresses, professionals or business owners.

Gentlemen and gentlewomen made up some 5 per cent of the population. They were landowners from established families, recognisable by coats of arms, upbringing or wealth. Priests ranked with this group.

About 200 gentlemen were knights. Originally, these were military officers, but by Tudor times, knighthood could be bestowed for civilian service. Gentlemen ran most of the palace departments. Sir Henry Guilford, for example, was the Comptroller of the Household. Gentlemen were carefully distinguished from yeomen, even if their functions might be similar.

The nobility were a very small group, no more than about forty lords and their families, as well as twenty-seven bishops. They were considered natural companions and councillors of the king. A few nobles had particular jobs at the top of the palace organisation. In the Eltham Ordinances, the Lord Steward was the Earl of Shrewsbury. Subsequently, Henry's friend the Duke of Suffolk was given the job, with the elevated title of 'Lord Great Master'.

The difference between ranks could be blurred. A bishop complained that because of the extravagant fashions at court 'a man cannot well discern a gentleman from a yeoman, a lord from a gentleman, a prince from a lord'. Laws called Acts of Apparel regulated what clothes and materials different classes could wear.

Many servants at the palace wore livery, essentially uniform coats. The servants of the king's chamber, including the Yeomen of the Guard, wore red livery, decorated with the royal cipher 'HR' in black and gold. Some of the lower-ranking servants wore green livery, the colour of the Tudor dynasty.

The members of staff had to be 'honest in gesture and behaviour' and expert in their jobs. The Vice-Chamberlain and the Captain of the Guard appraised the staff of the chamber, while the Comptroller of the Household had the oversight of the bulk of the staff. They had to replace any who were 'impotent, fickle, unable or unmeet'. The king wanted servants able and willing to progress, who behaved and looked the part. His household was 'a mirror and example to all others within this realm'.

CHAPTER 3

A Day at the Tudor Palace

6 a.m. The King's Chambers

In a world where people usually worked according to the length of daylight, the Tudor Palace ran to the regular pace of mechanical clocks. Towards the end of Henry VIII's reign, a gigantic astronomical clock was installed at Hampton Court. This was the work of the king's clock-maker, Nicholas Oursian, who also provided portable clocks. In the Privy Chamber there was a clock on a carved pillar.

The earliest risers were the king's personal attendants. They were expected to be up and ready at 7 o'clock in the morning, or earlier if the king had decided the night before that he would need an early start. In 1520, for example, Henry rose daily at 4 or 5 a.m., and hunted until 9 or 10 at night.

Getting up for 7 meant, for much of the year, working by the light of expensive wax candles. This was an expense Tudors generally liked to avoid. The rest of the court rose later and finished earlier to make the best use of daylight.

Next up were the four grooms of the Privy Chamber. They were named in the Ordinances as William and Hyrcan Brereton, Walter Welsh and John Cary. Personal servants would often be found sleeping in the same chamber as their master. Although Henry's grooms were assigned lodging elsewhere in the palace, at least two of them were to be ready and waiting in the Privy Chamber between 6 and 7 o'clock in the morning. They had to clear away the pallets (the straw mats on which staff had been sleeping), make the fire, tidy the room, strew clean straw on the floor and clean out 'all manner of filthiness'. When the king got up he would 'find the said Chamber pure, clean, wholesome and meet without any displeasant air or thing, as the health, commodity and pleasure of his most noble person doth require'.

Henry had a morbid fear of diseases, and fires were thought to dispel harmful vapours. Protective medicinal smells were introduced daily. Fires in the King's Chambers burnt expensive 'sea coal' – that is coal transported from the North of England by sea. Elsewhere in the palace, fires were fuelled by wood, readily available but more smoky and erratic.

There was a temptation for the highborn grooms to get their own servants to do the work for them. This was strictly forbidden. The king expected to be served by the designated staff, not by 'mean persons' substituting for them.

The single 'chamber' of the Middle Ages was replaced in Tudor times by a succession of chambers. The Eltham Ordinances refer to various 'outward chambers'. Rules relating to 'the King's Chamber' seem to apply indifferently to these rooms unless more detail is specified. How many there were depended on the size of the palace. At Hampton Court the number was continually increased. By the end of his reign, Henry had a sequence of chambers, starting with the one now known as 'the Great Watching Chamber', then a Presence

Chamber, followed by a Dining Chamber or Chamber of Estate.

Beyond was the Privy Chamber, the king's main living room. This led to the bedchamber itself. At Hampton Court this boasted an enormous bed 8ft long by 7ft 6in wide. Its four posts and head were carved, gilded and topped with vanes, and it was covered by a canopy and tester (a rear curtain) of cloth of gold and silver. Its curtains were of purple and white taffeta, decorated with the royal arms. It is not known if the king actually slept in this bed: more likely, it was a ceremonial object used, perhaps, when the king was ill and had to consult his ministers while still in bed. At the time of the Eltham Ordinances, there had only been one bedchamber for the king at Hampton Court. When the king extended the apartments, he added a second bedchamber, which is where he actually slept, in a sumptuous but more comfortable bed.

In the Privy Chamber, the king's personal staff gathered, waiting for the king to get up. The king's barber was present with his water, cloths, knives, combs and other equipment. He had not only to keep his own body and clothes clean, he had also to be a man of good character, not given to 'resorting to the company of vile persons or misguided women' to whom he might gossip about the confidences he might learn. The king, like the fashionable young men of the court, favoured a beard and moustache but his hair trimmed short. More conservative courtiers preferred collar-length hair and were clean-shaven.

One or both of the gentlemen ushers of the Privy Chamber (Roger Ratcliffe and Anthony Knevitt) had to be on hand by 7 a.m. to keep the door and ensure that no unauthorised persons came through. They also oversaw the work of the lesser servants. Next in rank were the pages of the King's Chamber, who were well-born sons of gentlemen. They would light the fires in the King's Chambers and warn the Esquires of the King's Body that it was time to get up, so that they could be ready to serve the king by 8 a.m. at the latest.

All six gentlemen of the Privy Chamber (in the Ordinances, they are Sir William Tiler, Sir Thomas Cheyney, Sir Anthony Browne, Sir John Russell,

Mr Henry Norris and Mr Cary) had to be ready in the Privy Chamber by 7 a.m. to dress the king. Two of them would have spent the night sleeping on pallets in the room. The clothes the king had decided to wear would be brought up from the ground-floor Wardrobe of the Robes by the yeoman of the Wardrobe of the Robes. The yeoman was not permitted to enter the Privy Chamber but handed the clothes over at the door to one of the grooms of the Privy Chamber.

The gentlemen of the Privy Chamber were the king's friends and companions. They would drink with him, gamble with him and share in his fun and games. They were very different from the unobtrusive servants of later Stately homes. Although they jealously guarded their privileged access to their royal friend, this did not prevent the king from passing time with the other servants. These were young men who shared much of the king's background and upbringing, his interests and passions.

At the first sound indicating that the king was actually awake, only one gentleman, Henry Norris, who had the senior role of groom of the stool, was allowed to enter the bedchamber 'and other privy places'. None of the others was to presume to enter or follow the king into the bedchamber or 'any other secret place'. What this meant was that the groom of the stool was responsible for helping the king go to the toilet – 'when he goeth to make water in his Bedchamber'. He would be ready with a basin of water, a ewer and towel for the King 'to wipe the nether end'. The toilet or 'Stool Room' was next to the bedchamber. It housed the close stool (hence 'groom of the stool'), a chamber pot set in a lidded casket covered in black velvet with padded arms and seat, scarlet sides with a gold fringe, decorated with 2,000 gold nails. The pot was of pewter. A water cistern, blanket, cotton or linen cloths were also provided.

The staff of the chamber at Hampton Court had the use of a built-in toilet or garderobe in a separate room off the Great Chamber. This was more convenient than chamber pots as it only required cleaning out periodically, when the court was away.

Alone with the groom of the stool, the king might go through his diary for the day. Once eased, he would be ready to go out into the Privy Chamber. The gentlemen would dress him in his chosen outfit 'in reverent, discreet and sober manner'. The grooms, holding the clothes, and the ushers on the door were absolutely forbidden, unless expressly commanded by the king, 'to lay hands upon his royal person, or inter-meddle with preparing or dressing of the same'. This was strictly the job of the gentlemen of the Privy Chamber.

Only the king and his immediate family could wear cloth of gold and the colour purple. Henry VIII was always the most splendidly dressed person at court. His clothes were made of the richest fabrics – such as silk brocades, taffeta, satin and velvet – and his shirts were of the finest quality embroidered linen. The inventory of the king's goods reveals that he had a large number of what were charmingly called 'babies', manikins dressed up in various suits of clothes to allow him to gauge the look of a particular outfit. There were large numbers of the king's very expensive trademark ostrich feathers, which were invariably added to the hat to complete the outfit.

In the intimate context of the Privy Chamber, confidences could be exchanged, and so opportunities for abuse of trust were always present. The Ordinances stressed that the men of the Privy Chamber should be 'loving together, and of good unity and accord, keeping secret all such things as shall be done or said in the same, without disclosing any part thereof to any person not being at the same time present in the said chamber'. Even if the king was absent, they had to wait diligently in the chamber, without gossiping about where he was or what he was doing and 'without grudging, mumbling or talking of the king's pastime, late or early going to bed or any other thing done by His Grace'. It was their duty to report anybody they overheard using 'any evil or unfitting language of the King'.

In the year following the issuing of the Eltham Ordinances, King Henry resolved to divorce Catherine of Aragon and marry Anne Boleyn. Six years later, Anne was on trial. Her light-hearted relationship with men of the Privy Chamber, including joking about the king's health and the size of his underwear, left

Anne and the gentlemen open to allegations of treason. Henry Norris and William Brereton were executed as part of the recriminations against her. Closeness to the king could bring extreme danger as well as opportunity.

The king, of course, could admit anyone he wanted into his own inner rooms – his councillors, sporting companions and friends. Wolsey's intention in the Ordinances was to regularise and limit the role of these 'minions', as they were called. Henry Courtney, Marquis of Exeter and Earl of Devon, 'the King's near kinsman ... brought up of a child with His Grace in the Chamber', was specifically named as someone who could come and go as a 'nobleman of the Privy Chamber', even though he had no particular job to do.

Gentlemen of the Privy Chamber were supposed to work six weeks on, six weeks off. As there was no strict rota, it sometimes happened that there would be no one present to serve the king. In such cases, Henry would summarily appoint another of his friends. The result was that, ten years later, the number of gentlemen had risen to sixteen.

The King's Chambers were situated on the first floor of the palace. We can be sure, though, that at ground level other essential departments of the palace were also stirring into life.

7 a.m. The kitchens

A typical day in the kitchens might begin as early as half past five. Conveniently, the staff slept either on pallets on the floors of their workplaces, known as 'offices', or in rooms directly above them.

Throughout the offices, fires were lit, including the great fireplace and ovens, charcoal stoves and boiling pots. Some of the offices were physically separate from the palace, forming a hinterland of buildings sprawling in front of the main gateway. Even those kitchens inside the palace were generally separated from the main rooms by a wide cloister that would serve as a fire break.

Feeding the royal household was one of the largest expenses the king faced. The Cofferer and the Comptroller, responsible for accounting, would open their books for the day. Would they need more supplies, and would they have to send to the Jewel House, where coin was kept, to pay suppliers?

The clerks of the kitchen would check the calendar. The 'red letter days' marked out the feasts of the Christian year. These would require more, larger and more elaborate dishes. Equally vital to observe were the fasting or 'fish' days. There were over 100 of these, comprising every Friday, the forty days of Lent, the twenty or so days of Advent, days before feasts and sometimes Wednesdays as well. Arcane laws governed what could be eaten on a fast day, but the absence of meat and restricted dairy products were common features, hence the reliance on fish.

Once the basic menu was established, preparations would start in earnest. Outside the palace proper, the men of the woodhouse would start chopping wood and delivering it to feed the fires. Brushwood was taken to the bakehouse to heat up the bread ovens. This had nineteen staff, led by the sergeant of the bakehouse. It included a privy bakehouse of two yeomen and two grooms, who made the exceptionally fine bread the king required. Once baked, the bread was delivered to the staff of the pantry inside the palace, who prepared it for issuing at meal times. As the principal 'vegetable' accompaniment to a Tudor meal, fresh bread was an absolute necessity.

Also outside were the scalding house, where birds were prepared for plucking, and the poultry house where they were made ready for cooking – notoriously unpleasant processes far away from the delicate noses of king and courtiers. In the rush house were stored the rushes used to cover floors and as cheap lighting.

Inside, the men of the coalhouse bagged up the charcoal for chafing dishes on which fine 'stove top' cookery would be performed. They also kept the sea coal that warmed the king and queen but which was too expensive for cooking.

The rooms used for storage, preparation, cooking and serving were all on the cooler, north side of the palace. Nevertheless, a Spanish nobleman who popped in while a meal was being prepared during the reign of Henry's daughter Mary described them as 'veritable hells', with all their noise and heat.

Candles, tapers and table linen were the province of the chaundry. In the winter months, a sufficient supply of lights was needed for the early risers, which added to the fire hazard of the kitchens.

The pastry house produced 'coffins' or pie cases, and it was here that pastry was made in long wooden kneading troughs. It was a very hot room, with four ovens heated by brushwood. The pastry served both the king and the court. Flour was stored here too, but other ingredients were usually stored separately, in larders that were under lock and key. The acatry was the office responsible for buying and storing meat and fish. Its clerks checked the orders to make sure everything was correct with no chance for fraud, and that stores were sufficient to requirements: only then would the clerks unlock the larders and the grooms carry the ingredients out to the kitchens.

The flesh larder stored butchered meat and hung game. Meat made up three-quarters of a courtier's diet. In one year, the court consumed 1,250 oxen, 8,200 sheep, 2,330 deer, 760 calves, 1,870 pigs and 53 boars.

The wet larder stored sea fish such as herring and cod in barrels of seaweed. The palace had its own supply of freshwater fish, carp, eels and pike (that came from its own ponds or moat), which would be kept here once caught.

The dry larder stored pulses and grains, which were generally used for thick stews called pottage, another vegetable accompaniment to meals.

The sergeant of the boiling house and his staff worked the 75-gallon capacity pans boiling stock and stews. Boiling meat was the most common form of preparation, but in the palace boiling yielded place to roasting. This was done in the Great Kitchen, where spits were turned on racks before the six huge fires. The Great Kitchen at Hampton Court is 40ft high, to aid ventilation, but the heat and smoke must have been tremendous nevertheless.

A more refined office was the confectory, where cooks made sweetmeats, marzipans and custards, presumably for the higher members of court.

8 a.m. The court

Up in the King's Chambers, the men were ready for His Majesty to start the day. In the outermost chambers, the yeoman ushers and yeoman waiters, along with the grooms of the chamber, took their place. These were general servants, suitable to fetch and carry and run errands. A yeoman usher in red livery took his place at the chamber door. He was only to permit entry to those lords, knights, gentlemen and officers who were supposed to pass through. He knew most of this closed circle by sight, but he was to use his wisdom and discretion to decide which other 'honest personages' should be allowed in. In case of doubt, the Lord Chamberlain or Vice-Chamberlain would be summoned to give a definitive judgement.

Most of those attending the king were accustomed to be served by their own servants. If these were allowed access, the rooms would quickly fill up, especially if their masters decided to turn it into a competition of who could keep the most retainers. The yeoman usher, therefore, stopped any gentleman's page coming through, except to briefly pass a message on to his master then leave as quickly as possible. At Hampton Court these pages had their own chamber, next to the Great Chamber. A gap between the tapestries allowed them to peek through to see when their masters might need them.

A visitor described the Great Chamber at Hampton Court as being filled with Yeomen of the Guard dressed in red and bearing halberds, though whether this was a regular occurrence is not clear – in the Ordinances their domain is the hall. In 1539 security was bolstered by the establishment of a bodyguard of fifty gentlemen pensioners, plus a captain, lieutenant and standard bearer, on a rota of which between ten and twelve were on duty at any time.

Knowing that the king rose early, guests and courtiers understood how important it was to be up and ready when he appeared. Attendance at court was vital for those who wanted to get on or obtain honours; being away meant not being able to know which way the king's mind was tending.

Assigning lodging to courtiers was the responsibility of the Lord Chamberlain (William Lord Sandys at the time of the Eltham Ordinances). There was little problem at Whitehall, where most courtiers owned or could rent houses in London and Westminster. Out in the country, they were dependent on the king's hospitality, however. Hampton Court included a whole range of courtiers' lodgings set around Base Court.

One hundred named individuals were allowed private accommodation. Base Court included twenty-seven double and thirteen single lodgings. Double lodgings, with a living room and separate bedroom, were the most sought after. They were allocated to ladies of the Queen's Privy Chamber, the chief gentleman of the Privy Chamber and other well-connected individuals, including at one point Lady Margaret Douglas (the king's niece), Lady Mary, the Master of the Horse and Thomas Cromwell (Lord Privy Seal).

There were ten more lodgings outside the gate, in the gardens. Obviously, this was not enough, so the Lord Chamberlain must have hoped that not everyone would turn up at once, or that some could be persuaded to share.

The courtiers had 'lads and other rascals' to keep their chambers for them. These had to be presented individually to the Comptroller, who would assess whether they were honest persons 'of good stature, gesture and behaviour'.

The Base Court lodgings were the last word in Tudor comfort. They had fireplaces and their own garderobes. Every chamber had a washbasin and a ewer of silver or gilt, a pot of wine or beer, a silver drinking bowl or goblet, a silver candlestick or two, with different sizes of candle. There was nothing to stop the courtiers modifying their own lodgings. The Marquis of Exeter brought more rushes, as well as hooks and cord to hang up his own tapestries and a tester for his bed.

Courtiers would dress in the finest way acceptable, subject to the Acts of Apparel. Velvet, silks and the finest linen were the favourite fabrics of the lords and ladies. Deep colours, including black, were signs of expense. Lower-ranking gentry were dressed in more ordinary fabrics such as wool, with fewer decorations. Portraits show courtiers wearing collars and badges expressing their allegiance to the Tudor house. The Comptroller of the Household, for instance, is shown wearing the collar of the Order of the Garter.

Meanwhile, preparations for meals continued. The king and queen had their own privy kitchens, below their Presence or Dining Chambers, catering for their individual needs. The king's was staffed by specialist French cooks. The royal doctors might prescribe particular diets for medical conditions: for example, the king was put on a very strict diet, combined with a regimen of physical fitness, for his 1540 marriage (two marriages, as it turned out).

9 a.m. The queen rises

Henry VIII can hardly be described as having a 'typical' queen. Each had a distinct personality, which clearly influenced the court to which she belonged. There were, however, formal aspects of queenship that did not depend exclusively on the individual woman.

The queen's apartments, known prosaically as 'the queen's side', were very much her domain. They were similarly configured to the king's. A Watching Chamber led to a Presence or Dining Chamber, which included a throne and canopy, with a private oratory, a Privy Chamber with hangings, cushions and tables, then a bedchamber. At the end of the queen's side, a Jewel House or private closet linked the king's and queen's apartments.

The staff was organised in line with those of the King's Chamber. The ladies of the Privy Chamber were married women, who were companions and personal servants like the king's gentlemen. Gentlewomen were similar to the gentleman ushers, while maids and chamberers were female equivalents to the grooms and pages. Young company was provided by the six maids of honour, the unmarried girls. They were supervised by the 'Mother of the Maids', under Anne Boleyn a Mrs Marshall, responsible for their education and guardianship. When the ladies of the Privy Chamber discovered that Anne of Cleves thought a kiss from the king in the evening and the morning was sufficient to get her pregnant, they advised her to chat to Mrs Lowe, the mother of her Dutch (German) maid to find out the facts of life.

Other jobs were filled by men, so there were male ushers, pages, cooks, tailors and a physician. The queen's household was headed by her Chamberlain (under Anne Boleyn Lord Burgh) with a Vice-Chamberlain (Sir Edward Baynton, who served Anne and all the later wives). She also had a chancellor, master of horse, secretary, receiver general and chaplains. How much supervision the queen herself gave depended on her own personality. Anne Boleyn, for instance, summoned a council of her household officers as soon as she became queen, and formally directed them in their duties.

As the king's early rising was sufficiently unusual to be remarked on, we can imagine the queen arising somewhat later, in natural daylight. Perhaps she would spend some time in bed before getting up, possibly with some bread and wine as a breakfast. Some of the ladies and the gentlewomen slept in the Privy Chamber, where there were six close stools for their use. Others had ground-floor or Base Court lodgings from which they would emerge to serve the queen.

Chamberers or ushers would bring up clothes from the Wardrobe of the Queen's Clothes, below her chambers. The king had particular styles of clothing that he liked to see his women wearing, and the queen would have the choice of the royal fabrics. She would decide which combination of sleeves and 'foreparts' would go best with a gown, which jewels to wear and whether to finish the outfit by covering her hair with a round French hood or a pointed English one. It was noted of Anne Boleyn that 'every day she made some change in the fashion of her garments'.

The ground floor of the queen's side contained a nursery, for use if the queen had a very young child. If the child lived, they would be allocated their own rooms. By the end of Henry's reign, Prince Edward had a suite of rooms similar to those of his father and stepmother, with a guard chamber, presence chamber, bedroom and bathroom with a garderobe. He even had his own privy kitchen beneath his rooms. When he was younger, one of the rooms was designated a 'rocking room' for his cradle.

As it was now daylight, the artificial lights could be extinguished. The king and queen's groom porters would go through the Chambers, collecting all the leftover torches and candles from the previous night. They brought the fragments down to the clerks of the spicery. Beeswax for candles was expensive and was hence counted among the spices. The clerks ensured that only the best quality was used at the palace, not mixed with any tallow (animal fat). They had to record how much was issued and how much returned. As well as wax and (obviously) spices, the office of the spicery was responsible for providing fruit, whether purchased or picked in the orchards.

It was up to the gentlemen ushers to work out how much wax, tapers, wood and coal the king and queen's chambers would require per day, and order the groom porters to fetch what was necessary.

The Chapel Royal

Religious observance was very much a part of life in the Tudor palace. On an ordinary day King Henry would make his devotions in private. Leading off the Privy Chamber was the king's Privy Closet or 'kneeling place'. This was a sumptuously furnished room with carpets, cushions and a kneeling desk. Next to it, with a grille between, was the small private chapel. The clerk of the closet or one of his two Privy Chaplains would say Mass. Henry had a great interest in religion, as befitted a man the pope had dubbed 'Defender of the Faith' and who then went on to claim the title of Supreme Head of the

Church of England on Earth. He would have had no difficulty following the service and readings in Latin. For him, this time must have been a welcome moment of quiet reflection and privacy away from the court.

The religious life of the queens was so varied that it is impossible to generalise. They had their own oratories and chaplains, while some, like Catherine Parr, might have been happier to read some devotional material for themselves. It is difficult to imagine Catherine Howard spending much time in her chapel.

On a Holy Day, Henry would process through his outer chambers to the Chapel Royal, the route filled with courtiers anxious to catch a glimpse of him. Yeomen of the Guard lined the route to keep order. Instead of entering the chapel at ground-floor level, he had a first-floor 'Holy Day Closet'. This was quite a large room, with bay windows looking down on the chapel.

The Chapel Royal functioned throughout the day. It opened with Matins at daybreak, proceeding through Lauds and Prime, with a High Mass followed by a shorter 'Lady Mass', devoted to the Virgin Mary, before noon. Generally, these ceremonies would take place in private, without the attendance of the courtiers, although Anne Boleyn directed all her staff to attend chapel daily.

The Chapel Royal had a very large staff, headed by the Dean, Richard Sampson. The gospeller and the epistoller chanted the readings for the day, ten boy choristers (led by the Master of the Children) sang the high parts and twenty gentlemen of the Chapel Royal the low parts. A verger and two yeomen looked after the building. In spite of all the religious changes in Henry's reign, the Chapel Royal remained an island of Catholic practice. The Mass was conducted with all the ceremony attendant on the belief that at the consecration the bread and wine literally became the body and blood of Christ. The services were conducted in Latin. There is no evidence that the law requiring the English version of the Bible was observed in the Chapel Royal, although the educated courtiers would have found it just as easy to understand Latin.

Only on feast days would the main body of the chapel be crammed with staff and courtiers. It was quite usual for members of the congregation to transact business, pausing only to kneel and cross themselves at the elevation of the Host. There were few occasions for them to join in. All fifty-two Sundays were feast days, but Saturdays were ordinary working days. There were about fifty other feast days scattered throughout the year. A side effect of the religious changes in Henry's reign was a reduction in the number of holidays, as reformers removed 'superstitious' feasts from the calendar.

Although feast days tended to be spent at a palace rather than a smaller residence, they were unusual occurrences. We shall assume our typical day is a 'ferial', or non-feast day.

On the hunt

Once the king had heard Mass, he was ready to enjoy himself. In his youth, jousting was his prime leisure activity. There were tiltyards at Greenwich and Hampton Court, and sometimes at Whitehall. After two serious accidents, which left his legs badly damaged, he gave up this activity in favour of non-contact sports. He enjoyed hawking and falconry, sports for late summer and early autumn. There is no doubt, however, that on a 'typical' day at the palace it is hunting that would have occupied his time: Henry often rose earlier than the official timetable to make sure there was enough time for hunting. In the 1540s, for instance, he rose at 6 a.m., heard Mass at 7 then left immediately afterwards.

All the palaces, other than Whitehall, were surrounded by large hunting parks. Early in the morning, huntsmen would be out in the park singling out suitable quarry for the king: perhaps a great buck, a male fallow deer, solitary with more than twelve tines on its antlers, an eye-catching beast. The huntsmen would isolate the quarry, stationing themselves around it to direct its flight once the hunt began.

The palaces had several stables, at a distance from the main building. The majority of horses were used to transport the court or the personal property of the courtiers. There were strict limitations on how many horses a courtier could have. The king's own horses were partitioned away from the common stables. The Master of the Horse, Sir Nicholas Carew, was a senior officer.

He would know the king's requirements and make sure there were sufficient suitable horses. There were, for instance, thirty 'great horses' used for war and tournaments, which were extremely expensive to buy and maintain. For hunting, the king required faster, lighter horses called coursers, of appropriate size for his height and bulk.

The grooms, who lived above the stables, would have the animals groomed and tacked up, at the command of the Master of the Horse. The king usually tired out eight to ten horses on a hunt. The Master of the Horse would take care to have remounts stationed beforehand at intervals along the route, so that as the king tired one horse he could change to another. The king's first horse and those of his party would be brought into the palace courtyard, saddled and ready. A great stair led directly down to the courtyard from the king's lodgings, for his convenience. A mounting block would be positioned at the foot of the stairs, with grooms to hold his horse and help him onto it.

The king was said to be especially amenable when setting off on a hunt. This inevitably meant that the courtyard would be filled with suitors. Nobles who had been summoned to the court (an ominous sign) might seek to assure him of their loyalty.

The Ordinances noted that, 'because heretofore, whensomever the King's Grace hath gone further in walking, hunting, hawking or other disports, the most part of the noblemen and gentlemen of the court have used to pass with His Grace', the court had ended up empty and the king's 'disports' had been spoilt by too many hangers-on:

It is therefore the King's pleasure and straight commandment that no person of what estate, degree or condition soever he be, do from henceforth presume to pass before or after the King's Highness, at his said time of disport, but such only as by the King's commandment shall be appointed and warned from time to time by one of the gentlemen ushers of the King's Privy Chamber or some other person of the same.

Catherine of Aragon, and then Anne Boleyn, often hunted with the king. The queen had her own stable, where her horses were kept. It seems, though, that the king was unusually fond of the sport, so in this typical day we will imagine the queen remaining at the palace while her husband hunts.

The king would have his pick of companions, perhaps Henry Norris or some of the other gentlemen of the Privy Chamber. His closest companion was probably Charles Brandon, who married one of his sisters and became Duke of Suffolk and Lord Great Master of the Household. Other high-ranking lords who enjoyed the king's favour might include the dashing young Earl of Surrey, cousin to Anne Boleyn and Catherine Howard, the Marquis of Exeter, the king's closest kinsman, and, perhaps, a brother of the current queen. The king liked to joke and boast, matching wit with his friends. Courtiers could not rely on the king's friendship, though. Exeter, Surrey, Norris and Anne Boleyn's brother, Lord Rochford, all ended their days on the scaffold, victims of the king's displeasure.

As the hunting party trotted out through the palace gates, their horses' shod hooves clattering on the cobbles, they would be met by the hounds and their handlers. The hounds were kept in kennels outside the palace, separated by breed and function. If the quarry was a fallow buck, it would be the task of the green-liveried master of the buckhounds and his grooms to have the appropriate dogs ready for the chase.

Orders would be taken to the king's Privy Kitchen that the king would dine away from court and suitable dishes would be prepared. The food could be taken to the park in hampers by mounted couriers. The master of the revels would have to sort out tents in case the party wanted to eat under cover. In the kitchens, the sergeant of the squillery and his officers would buff up the vessels of pewter and silver in which the food for the court would soon be served.

10 a.m. Dining in the Great Hall

Tudors expected their dinner, their main meal, around midday. In the palace, however, this was simply not practical for everyone. The Great Hall had a capacity of 300 or so, but it would require two sittings for everyone who had the right to eat there to do so. The number of diners meant that the first sitting had to start at 10 a.m., or sometimes earlier.

The master cooks would check that the meat was good, sweet, and well dressed, before serving it out at the dressers, small rooms where the food was prepared for presentation. Here, the clerk of the green cloth would view the food to confirm that it was properly prepared 'wholly, entirely and in due proportion' for the correct destination. The clerks of the kitchen were also on hand to check that the quality of the finished product was such as tended to the king's 'most honour and profit'. Once approved, the food passed through hatches to servants in the serving place to be taken upstairs.

Great Halls were quite rare. That at Hampton Court was the last the king had built. Nonsuch, his only completely new palace, did not include a Great Hall. The splendid tapestries that now hang in the Great Hall of Hampton Court were not regular decorations. They would be brought out from storage only on grand cere-monial occasions, when the hall came under the control of the Lord Chamberlain, essentially as a glorified outer chamber to the King's Chambers beyond.

On a typical day, the hall came under the Lord Steward, with its own staff of marshals, sergeants, sewers and surveyors. It acted as a dormitory during the night. Once the pallets were cleared away, it became a common room for men like the harbingers and messengers, as well as musicians and entertainers who were not part of the household.

Once the food was ready, sergeants would set up trestle tables and bring benches out from store. White linen tablecloths would cover the tables. These would run down either side of the hall, with a third on the dais at the end furthest from the serving entrances.

Communal meals encouraged friendship and loyalty to the king. When hall was kept, food and drink were not to be served in other chambers except as allowed by custom, for instance to the kitchen staff. The king was fighting a losing battle to stem the obsolescence of the Great Hall. The Ordinances bemoan the fact that with the hall so seldom kept there ensued a 'lack of good knowledge, experience and learning, how young men should order themselves in the execution of their offices' and household servants put on board wages instead 'give themselves many times to idleness, evil rule and conversation'.

The marshals would check that the people entering were entitled to eat in hall. Attached to the Eltham Ordinances was a list called 'Bouche of Court' specifying exactly who was allowed to dine at the king's expense. A large number of those dining in hall were Yeomen of the Guard. One of the main intentions of the Ordinances was to reduce this force down to 100 – an initiative commanded by the Vice-Chamberlain. In all, about 600 people had Bouche of Court, including 230 domestic servants expected to eat elsewhere, but this number was open to extension.

Food would be served at the tables by sewers, overseen by the surveyors. It is likely that the marshals allocated the seating and perhaps varied the dishes according to rank, giving senior staff members, knights and gentlemen, ladies and priests, seats at the high table on the dais. There would be two main courses for the diners, consisting of a variety of dishes they could choose from.

Dishes would be allocated to 'messes' of four to six men, who would serve themselves, taking food from the serving vessels to their own plates, probably pewter trenchers. Each member of the household had a substantial beer and wine allowance. Three hundred barrels of beer (about 2.5 million litres) were consumed a year – enough for about twelve pints per person per day. Drinking vessels were generally made of pewter, though some horn and leather cups might have been in evidence. Mutton was the main dish of the household. Between 80 and 100 sheep carcasses were consumed a day, with chet, bread from coarse flour, the main accompaniment. Pottage, a thick soup made of vegetables such as leeks and onions, herbs, oatmeal, garlic and stock, was a common dish, and mustard the main condiment.

In the hall, diners would probably provide their own knives and spoons to eat with, although food was taken to the mouth in the fingers: it was therefore important that bowls of water and napkins were provided for washing hands

Dinners were taken at a leisurely pace, but there must have been pressure on those at the first sitting to finish within an hour to allow the tables to be cleared for the next shift.

Food waiting to be served would be set out in 'leaning places' next to the hall. There was always the risk it could go missing, either through outright theft or by staff taking advantage of 'fees' (perks) of untouched food, lees of wine or crusts cut off bread before serving. Some had a lucrative sideline selling these on. The sewers and surveyors had to ensure that no food set forth from the dresser ended up being purloined, taken away or embezzled.

For those who needed to relieve themselves after dinner, but without the convenience of their own garderobes, there was a public toilet called 'the Common Jakes' just outside the main entrance. It had two storeys, each with fourteen seats, which were just circular holes in wooden boards. The waste discharged directly into the Thames. The jakes also served as a facility for visitors and for those lodged outside the palace. But there must always have been the temptation, with the amount of beer drunk, not to walk so far but to avail oneself of whatever secluded place was at hand: the inhabitants of the palace were admonished to 'beware the emptying of piss-pots and pissing in chimneys'. The Eltham

Ordinances forbade 'nuisance in court . . . no person of what degree soever shall make water or cast any annoyance within the precinct of the court, within the gates of the porter's lodge, whereby corruption may breed and tend to the prejudice of his royal person'. At Greenwich Palace, large red crosses were painted on the plaster 'that none should piss against them'. There were outdoor stone and lead urinals placed in the courtyards at the foot of the stairs to the king and queen's lodgings.

Hygiene was a very important consideration at the palaces. The courtiers' garderobes in Base Court connected with the main palace drains. These ran down to the river, passing under the water-filled moat. This avoided polluting the moat and filling the palace with unpleasant smells, not to mention safeguarding the fish for human consumption. Where the garderobes could not connect to the drains, they emptied into large pits that were cleaned out between visits of the court by Philip Long (the master scourer) and his team of gong scourers, boys or small men who could go down to empty them by hand.

While the first sitting ate, others carried on with their business. On the ground floor, below the King's Chambers, Sir Brian Tuke, treasurer of the chamber, paid the officers of the Privy Chamber.

The Lord Steward's department was more rigid. The three senior officers, the Lord Steward, Treasurer and Comptroller – known as 'White Sticks' from the white staves they carried as signs of rank – were responsible for budgeting expenditure. There were constant alterations to try to make the system watertight. When the office of Lord Steward was abolished, the new 'Lord Great Master' inherited all his powers and responsibilities, as well as authority over the Lord Chamberlain.

In practice, these great men probably left the day-to-day work to their junior officers, the clerks of the green cloth and the clerk comptrollers. They were encouraged to make daily inspections of the larder and twice-weekly inspections of the offices and chambers at meal times, to see if there were any strangers eating there.

Officers made a daily report to the clerks of the Board of Green Cloth. This was actually a table covered with a green cloth, on which the clerks did their accounts by moving bone counters in the manner of an abacus. At Hampton Court, the Board of Green Cloth was set up conveniently in a room above the main service entrance to the palace, so the clerks could easily check deliveries. The Cofferer kept a daily check on the household's budgets, estimates and expenditure.

11 a.m. Dining in the chamber

It was now time for the second sitting to be held in hall, and for the chambers to be set up for those privileged to dine there. As with the lower servants, it was important for the king that the higher courtiers should not dine separately 'in corners or secret places' leaving the head officers of the household 'destitute of company at their boards'. This would impair the good order of the house-hold and lead to waste. None of the nobles, councillors or office holders was permitted to eat meals elsewhere, unless they ate afterwards with the gentlemen of the Privy Chamber.

If the king was not eating in his Dining Chamber, that room would have a table set up for lords spiritual and temporal 'to be served with the service called the King's service'. Barons or higher would dine here, the table presided over by a lord of the rank of earl.

The Great Chamber was where senior staff such as the Lord Chamberlain, Vice-Chamberlain, Captain of the Guard, Master of the Horse, Lord Steward, Comptroller and the Cofferer dined, with lesser ranking councillors and barons, along with such gentlemen as were invited and strangers (foreigners) who happened to be in the court. The Lord Steward's men sat at separate messes from the Lord Chamberlain's.

Because some palaces had more chambers than others, it is not always possible to be precise about which were used for dining. Some accounts describe eating in the Presence Chamber, rather than the Great and Dining Chambers. The imperial ambassador, Chapuys, described how, on Easter Day, he had turned up to the chamber at 6 a.m. for a chance to see the king. He was received by the Lords of the Council in the Presence Chamber. The king briefly acknowledged him as he went through on his way to Mass, but Chapuys was again left hanging around until he was invited to dine there 'with all the principal men of the court'.

The visiting Duke of Najera described the Presence Chamber at Whitehall as being filled with nobles, knights and gentlemen, with a canopy (the Cloth of Estate) and chair of rich figured brocade. No one would dare to stand under the Cloth of Estate. The canopy at Hampton Court was embroidered with the words '*Vivat Rex Henricus Octavus*' (Long Live King Henry VIII) in pearls.

Food was served with ceremony by servants in red livery. They would wait in the leaning place before making a colourful entrance as each dish was announced. Platters were placed on sideboards ready to serve.

Meals in the chambers would be copious, with much variety. As in the hall, there would be two courses served to messes of four. There were prime cuts of expensive meat like beef, game and unusual birds, perhaps dressed with their feathers. Servants would wash the diners' hands before and between courses. The gentry were well aware of the strict rules governing table etiquette, and so diners would have clean fingernails and would not presume to wipe their knives on a neighbour's clothes or lean their elbows on the table. They would convey small morsels of meat, cut from the bone, to their mouths, no larger than would allow them to swallow promptly and reply when addressed. Ale, beer and wine would be drunk out of silver or gilt goblets, or perhaps from Venetian glass. A similar amount of wine to ale (twelve pints) was allocated per person per day, but it was served to far fewer people, which explains much about the behaviour of members of the court. A Spanish visitor in Mary's reign said that the courtiers drank more than would fill the Valladolid river, ascribing the 'great goings on' at the palace to the fact that ladies and gentlemen sugared their wine.

Meat was carved and served on gold or silver plates. Hot and cold sauces accompanied the dishes, served on shallow rimless dishes called saucers. Apples and pears from the orchard varied the diet. The main accompaniment was manchet, a delicate white bread. Salt would be available on the table in an expensive vessel, but was locked away after the meal. Identical sets of spoons and knives were probably provided, though a noble might bring his own to shown off their design or materials.

12 noon. Relaxation

The kitchen staff would finally be able to sit down to eat in their own offices. As they were actually responsible for the food it is quite likely that, while being a long way down the pecking order and excluded from dining in hall, they might be in a position to ensure some of the more exotic dishes were available for their own consumption.

The courtiers would now take the opportunity to relax. The Duke of Najera was entertained by Queen Catherine's brother and another noble before they were shown into the King's Chamber, but even then did not see the king.

Perhaps the large dinner would settle best with a light walk. New features of the Tudor palaces, on both the king's and queen's sides, were galleries, running alongside the private rooms. These were places for the king and queen to walk when the weather was not good enough to go outside. They were furnished with tables, forms and stools and hung with pictures, tapestries and mirrors. For preference, it seems that conversations were held outside.

A private staircase ran directly from the junction of the king's and queen's sides down to their Privy Garden. The Privy Gardens at Whitehall and Hampton Court were a series of compartments, like outdoor rooms, decorated with carved royal beasts bearing shields and vanes. Each compartment had a sundial, so that the walkers would not lose track of time. Thomas Chapman was the gardener at Hampton Court, but women did the weeding and watering, being paid 2 pence a day as against 6 pence a day for men. Perhaps Alice Brewer and Margaret Rogers, paid for gathering strawberries, primroses and violets at Hampton Court, were among these women gardeners.

Encounters in the gardens and galleries were ideal opportunities for ladies and gentlemen to socialise. Generally, there was a lively, light-hearted approach to personal morality at the court. For the upper classes, 'courtly love' provided a formalised framework for gallantry and flirtation. Ladies and gentlemen would exchange courtesies, wear tokens of love for each other, compose poems and so forth. There would be secret liaisons and pledges of love. Kissing was a usual, fulsome method of greeting, and many games such as chasing, blind man's buff and the like seem intended to facilitate physical contact. Anne Boleyn invited ladies and gentlemen to 'pastime in the Queen's chamber', including dancing. The talk turned to laughing at the king's clothes and his poetry, which was to have fatal consequences.

Meanwhile, new visitors would be arriving at the palace through the day. At Whitehall, when Parliament was sitting, the gates would be particularly busy with those anxious to influence the lawmakers. Even out of term, there would be many seeking entrance. There were the queen and the Councillors to influence, to ensure favourable positioning when the king returned. Every door brought a new porter or usher to be bribed, coaxed or browbeaten into letting the visitor past. Begging letters would be delivered by courier for those not able to make the trip, or perhaps smoothing the way for a later visit with gifts of food and drink.

At the entrance, the groom porter would check that there were not too many servants following their masters. The dukes and the archbishops were limited to twelve, the Lord Chamberlain to ten. Gentlemen of the Privy Chamber could have four servants but sergeants and clerks only one. Guards, heralds, messengers, minstrels, falconers, huntsmen or footmen could not retain any 'boys or rascals' to serve them.

Some would be summarily turned away. This meant that many pages would be found hanging around the gate ready to run errands for their masters. They could come in to bring them things such as drink, when required, but had to leave as soon as their job was done.

Serving the great was a means of educating young gentlemen. For this reason, the Councillors, the king's and queen's Chamberlains, Vice-Chamberlains, Captain of the Guard, Master of the Horse, and the gentlemen of the Privy Chamber could each have one page attendant on them, as an apprentice, providing they were 'gentlemen born, well mannered and apparelled, and well conditioned'.

It was part of the porter's job to ensure that food, candles, pots, firewood or the silver or pewter vessels for guests were not smuggled out. While the porter kept an eye out for unwanted humans, the dogkeeper got rid of unwanted dogs. Nobody of any degree was to keep greyhounds, mastiffs, hounds or other dogs in the court. Small dogs such as spaniels for the ladies were exempted. Jane Seymour is shown with a little dog sitting on the train of her dress in the Whitehall mural. Catherine Parr had a pet spaniel called 'Rig'.

Grooms would clear the table linen from the dining rooms and deliver it to the laundry. Here, five men under the yeoman launderer boiled the cloths and put them out to dry, inside, in front of braziers. The king's bedlinen and underclothes were laundered daily by his laundress Anne Harris, who provided her own soap and herbs to make them smell sweet.

1 p.m. Pastime with good company

Now their food had settled, it was time for the courtiers to get down to the serious business of enjoying themselves. The palaces were in many ways large sport and entertainment complexes. Tennis was a popular modern sport for courtiers. There were tennis plays, as the indoor courts were called, at Hampton Court, Richmond, Windsor and Woodstock. Tennis was a game in which only men would participate, but both male and female spectators would watch from the first-floor gallery and gamble on the outcome. It was a good option if the weather was bad. The game was fast, the scoring complex and inevitably tempers ran high. Sir Edward Knyvet struck another courtier on the nose during a game of tennis. He was sentenced to have his hand cut off, for violence within the Verge, and was only saved by the intervention of Queen Catherine Howard.

Bowls could be played either outdoors or indoors. Slower-moving than tennis, it still offered the attraction of gambling on the result. For more bloodthirsty entertainment, Whitehall had a cocking house where courtiers could set their cockerels to fighting. Archery targets called butts could be set up in the gardens to facilitate the national military pastime. Noblemen might even have a go at wrestling.

In the excitement generated by the sports, courtiers had to be careful not to let down their guard. There would always be informers eavesdropping to pass on even the most trivial of remarks. Lady Hussey was sent to the Tower for calling the king's eldest daughter 'the Princess' after she had been relegated to the status of 'Lady Mary'. Two of Anne of Cleves's ladies-in-waiting were jailed, after the death of Catherine Howard, for voicing what must have been a frequently asked question, 'How many wives will he have?'

While the courtiers took advantage of the facilities, the work of the palaces continued unabated. In the kitchens, supper was being prepared. Through the cloisters, corridors and courtyards, servants fetched food and drink and carried sporting equipment, including arms and hawks, out to the courtiers.

Nor did deliveries stop. Wheat, delivered by cart or by barge, would be checked by the sergeant of the bakehouse and his two purveyors to make sure that it was the best available and at the best price.

The porter, leaving one of his yeomen in charge on the gate, would lead the other four yeomen and two grooms on one of their periodic sweeps of the palace. They did this three or four times a day to expel intruders, or perhaps those who might not have been generous enough with their bribes on entering.

2 p.m. The king returns

Outdoor sports were not the way for female courtiers to fill their time. The ladies might repair to the Queen's Chambers for conversation. The normal and expected activity for ladies and their maids was needlework, sewing, embroidery and making clothes. The chambers of Anne Boleyn at Hampton Court were described as sumptuous, with 'rich and exquisite works for the greater part wrought by her own hand and needle, and also of her ladies'.

Outside, the sound of horns and the baying of hounds signalled the return of the king and his hunting party. No effort would have been spared to ensure that the hunt was successful. The bucks had already been butchered in the field, traditionally by the hunter himself. Their impressive carcasses, slung over the horses, would attract the admiration of those who had remained behind. There was no question of the venison being consumed immediately: it would be taken to the flesh larder to hang for six weeks before consumption.

The exhausted horses would be taken back to the stables to be tended to, where the king's avenor and his two clerks ensured there was enough fodder for them.

King Henry was a creature of whim, who had to have his own way and could not be bound by the regulations of the court. This being so, the gentlemen of the Privy Chamber had to have 'a vigilant and reverent respect and eye to His Grace, so that by his look or countenance, they may know what lacketh or is his pleasure to be had or done'. The ushers and grooms would stand waiting, at a convenient distance from the king, without presuming to approach other than to fulfil their duties.

Let us suppose he decided, as seems to have been quite usual, to take a bath to freshen up after the hunt. Henry had separate baths or bayne chambers in his palaces, by the bedchamber. They were served with hot and cold running water, the hot water warmed in a boiler in the adjacent room. Conduits and cisterns provided clean water to the palaces, with water brought in by pipe from springs. At Hampton Court, these were on the other side of the Thames and the pipes had to run under the river. Repair of pipes was a regular occurrence.

The bath itself was essentially half a large barrel, lined with linen cloths. Henry could relax, be cleaned and ease his aching legs, perhaps attended by the groom of the stool.

Things were not quite so easy for other courtiers who wished to bathe. Bathtubs, with a capacity of 30 gallons, would have to be brought from store to their lodgings. Hot water would have to be boiled over fires and laboriously emptied into the tub from earthenware vessels.

If the clothes the king had worn on the hunt required mending or cleaning, grooms would take them down to the Wardrobe of the Robes. These expensive garments would be dry cleaned, by brushing, use of fuller's earth or shearing off stained wool.

Supposing the king had some free time after his bath, he might repair to his study next door. His books were shelved in the library on the second floor but could be brought down for his convenience, as could jewels and other curios from the Jewel House. Henry kept numerous plats or designs for his palaces, which he might also peruse.

While the king was elsewhere, his Privy Chamber would be used as a common room 'without immoderate and continual play of dice, cards or tables [backgammon and other board games]', nor 'frequent and intemperate plays, as the Groom Porter's house'. This was a matter of degree, as the men were allowed 'honest and moderate play' of chess, tables and cards. The proviso was that as soon as they heard or saw that the king was on his way, they would stop playing and be ready to serve him.

The Privy Chamber men were not supposed to try to advance themselves, urge petitions, or meddle with 'causes and matters'. They were admonished to remember that the closer they were to the king's person, the more important it was for them to be humbly reverent, sober, discreet and serviceable. By this means alone they would deserve preferment. This way not only would their own honour increase but, more importantly, 'honour and wisdom may be ascribed to the King's Highness, that His Grace has so circumspectly chosen such well qualified, mannered and select persons to be nigh about and attendant upon his noble person'. We can see in these strictures how anxious Cardinal Wolsey was that this arrangement should not become an alternative source of patronage to his own. It would hardly be surprising if the household staff did not try to take advantage of the opportunities offered by their closeness to the king.

When Chapuys visited the court (remember, he had been waiting in the Presence Chamber since 6 a.m.), the king eventually came out to see the ambassador in the afternoon. He took him back into the Privy Chamber, followed by Thomas Cromwell and the Chancellor. Henry took Chapuys over to a window for a private chat, while Cromwell sat on a coffer and sent for a drink.

3 p.m. Business

We should not imagine that life at the palace was all play for the king and his court. Henry was very much the head of government, and he ruled from his palace. This meant that facilities for the Privy Council formed part of what were ostensibly the king's private chambers. A Council Chamber was located off the gallery.

The Privy Council consisted of about twenty 'honourable, virtuous, sad, wise, expert and discrete' men. They included office holders such as the Lord Chancellor, the Lord Chamberlain, the Lord Steward, Treasurer and Comptroller of the Household. Alongside them sat those personally valued by the king, together with men whose high rank guaranteed them a hearing regardless of office.

The Privy Councillors conducted business formally, sitting around a table. That is not to say that meetings were always sedate affairs. As tempers ran high, the king might curse his secretary, Thomas Cromwell, calling him a knave and beating him round the head. On another occasion, Lord Lisle jumped up and slapped Bishop Gardener of Winchester around the face.

If the king wanted bread or drink, one of the gentlemen ushers of the Privy Chamber would pass the order on to a groom of the Privy Chamber, who would rush down to the officers of the buttery, pantry or cellar, whichever it might be, to place the order. The officers would bring up the food to the door of the chamber. The ushers would test and perhaps taste it, then bring it in and place it on the cupboard and stand by to receive orders. It was the responsibility of the gentlemen of the Privy Chamber specifically to serve the king, and discharge the ushers.

The work of receiving deliveries would be continuing at ground level. Bulky cargoes would, where possible, be transported by barge and unloaded at wharves owned by the houses of offices. Ale and beer would be received on the wharf by men of the buttery. The purveyors would have to check that the barrels were of a true gauge and fully filled.

However they arrived, by barge, wagon or pack animal, foodstuffs would be taken to the larders through the service entrance, not the Great Gatehouse. The chief clerk of the kitchen and his underclerks checked that the food destined for the king was 'the best and sweetest stuff that could be got' and that for the other ranks in the household was good 'according to their degrees'. It had to be conveyed to the larders in good time for the cooks to use it, in this case ready for the first sitting of dinner the following day. Preparations for this day's supper would be almost completed by now.

Courtiers and guests with nothing else to do but wait for supper might have gone back to their own lodgings, with wine sent for their refreshment.

4 p.m. The children of the palaces

It was now time for the first sitting of supper in the hall. Apart from being, perhaps, slightly lighter than dinner, this would be very similar to the dining process already described. This is therefore an opportunity for an aside on the life of children at the palace.

The pages and maids at court were largely made up of young people – children in our view. The master of the henchmen was responsible for the education of the boys and the mother of the maids for the girls'.

As well as an education, the king's children required officers who mirrored roles in the adult court. Mary lived apart from her father's court from the time of the

Eltham Ordinances, though seldom less than 10 miles away, and she would often be present as a visitor. Lady Elizabeth was occasionally resident. The king's long-awaited son, Prince Edward, was allocated his own chambers. At the age of 2 he was assigned his own household under the Lady Mistress, Margaret Lady Bryan. He had a chamberlain and vice-chamberlain. When he reached the age of 7 his stepmother, Catherine Parr, provided him with fourteen boys of his own age as companions, to learn with him. Along with reading, writing in various languages, mathematics and science in formal lessons, the curriculum was enlivened with music, dancing and fencing. He was also allowed to take part in a non-contact version of jousting, running at the ring, which he would have to catch on the point of his lance.

In most ways, however, the fact that some inhabitants of the palace were children was scarcely acknowledged. They were expected to fit into an adult world in behaviour, dress and responsibility.

Vespers would be sung in the chapel about this time. The services were signalled by bells, which gave a structure to the day for those unable to see a clock or tell the time by one.

5 p.m. Diversions

As the second sitting of supper in the hall took place, those in the chambers beyond would seek some diversions while waiting for their own meals. There was no particular reason for Henry to stop the dice and board games going on in his Privy Chamber. His accounts show he lost around £100 a year in small change, to people of just about any rank. Lady Mary was equally happy to gamble away £2 a month. The fact that they lost at all (the accounts make no mention of winnings) shows that the wagers were real and that courtiers would not (always) lose in order to please their royal hosts.

With many temptations on offer and large quantities of alcohol consumed, it is not surprising that violent altercations would break out. The knight marshal might well be called upon to break up a fight over women below stairs.

Formal entertainments were a good way of channelling excess energy. The master of the revels was responsible for devising court shows and plays, for formal occasions. On a typical day, this meant that there would be scenery to be made and painted, costumes to be designed and fitted and lines to be learnt. The master of the children of the Chapel Royal, William Cornish had been very accomplished in coming up with all sorts of disguisings, presumably using his choristers. A famous such event, a mock combat around a fake fortress called Chateau Vert, had introduced Anne Boleyn to the king.

Entertainments required musical accompaniment. Formal occasions of whatever type could require musicians' services, too. There were sixteen trumpeters, primarily used to announce the king and visitors. One of them, John Blank, was the only known black resident in the palaces. Another thirty-four musicians, both men and women, were on the payroll.

6 p.m. Supper

Although in the hall men had been sitting down to supper for some time, the Tudors normally ate supper in the early evening, depending on how soon it got dark. As with dinner, the Great Chamber and Dining Room on both the king's and queen's sides would be transformed by grooms setting up trestle tables and benches.

As the king and queen had been apart for most of the day, supper might be an ideal time for them to meet. Henry typically began each of his marriages very affectionately. He would hardly be able to keep himself away from his wife. Usual protocol would be for the queen to invite the king to her chambers.

If the king decided to dine in the Dining Chamber, the Lord Chamberlain or the Vice-Chamberlain would attend him for as long as he required. Once they were released, a gentleman usher would wait on the king. No other men of the chamber were permitted to loiter unless the king specifically commanded it. Instead, the lords, knights, gentlemen, chaplains and so forth would return with the Lord Chamberlain and Vice-

Chamberlain to the Great Chamber to dine. The chamber would be set for food and the usher would show out all other persons except the sewers and grooms of the chamber and officers such as the butler, pantler, ewer and the restricted number of permitted servants (three for the Chamberlain, two for the Vice-Chamberlain, one for the Captain of the Guard). A yeoman usher on the door would make sure no others got in.

During the meal, a yeoman usher would pass up and down the chamber to see that good service and quiet order was maintained. The butler was responsible for making sure the diners had enough to drink. The usual practice was for wine to be poured as required, the butler and his grooms taking the vessel back to the cupboard between drinks. The pantler made sure that the diners had the bread they needed, while the ewer provided the water necessary for the diners to wash their hands after picking up the food.

Waiting areas, called haute-paces, outside chamber doors, were notorious places for 'all manner of servants, rascals and boys' to hang around. An indication of this can be seen at Hampton Court where, in a window sill in the corridor beside the Great Chamber, someone has used their knife to carve out the board for the popular game 'Fox and Geese'. The haute-paces had to be cleared out by the yeoman waiters. These officers also had to make sure that no ale, water, broken meat or any other refuse carried from the King's Chambers should lie around there.

On one occasion, when Anne Boleyn invited Henry to supper in her own rooms, the chambers were described as hung with the best tapestries and the tables set with gold plate. Even at a private supper there would generally be several guests, including the queen's ladies and individuals agreeable to the king and queen such as the Duke of Suffolk and the Lord Chancellor.

The carver and server of the king's food would be noblemen. The king would be served first, wherever he was, then the other guests in order of rank. These meals were a chance for the French cooks of the Privy Kitchen to show off their virtuosity. There would be rare and exotically presented dishes such as 'Peacock Royale', where the birds were served in feathered skins with gilded beaks and feet. 'Subtleties' (confections) – for example an edible chessboard with edible chessmen – would delight the sophisticated diners. These were often made from marchpane (ground almonds, sugar and rosewater). Other deserts included roses, marigolds, gilliflowers, violets and rosemary preserved in sugar syrup, and imported fruits, perhaps candied.

The king's wine was kept in a cellar under the Great Chamber. Beside it was a drinking house for the sergeant of the cellars to test the quality. French wine was the most favoured. Wine could be spiced, as was *Ypocras*, which was flavoured with cinnamon, sugar, cloves, nutmeg and pepper.

Because the gentlemen, ushers and grooms of the Privy Chamber were first and foremost the king's servants and 'it is not convenient that any certain time be prefixed for the King's going to dinner or to supper', it was acknowledged that they might not be able themselves to observe the fixed hours for eating. In order that they should not miss out on their free meals, one mess of meat was prepared for the grooms and the barber and two for the gentlemen and the ushers, set aside by the ushers in some convenient place, so they could be served it when they were able. This was prepared by the king's Privy Kitchen, honestly and well dressed. 'If it shall fortune the King's Highness to go forth on his hunting and disports and shall for his pastime and well accompanying of his person, call more gentlemen than the said six . . . a substantial proportion of two other messes of meat' would be made in the Privy Kitchen. If the king did not return in time for dinner 'the same may be dressed and served unto them' in the company of the gentlemen.

7 p.m. Music and dancing

Once supper was over and the tables cleared away, the king and queen might conclude the evening with music and dance. Henry was known for his songs, new compositions and adaptations. He sang in a fashionably high voice, rather unexpected for his height and bulk. He played several different musical instruments, including the organ, the virginals and the recorder. He also encouraged his friends and family to do the same. Mary and Elizabeth, for example, played the lute. Doubtless, the queen and her guests were delighted by his displays of virtuosity.

Not all the entertainment was provided by the guests themselves. The queen retained six minstrels of her own, who might accompany a dance or provide soothing 'background' music. One of Anne Boleyn's virginals players, Mark Smeeton, was seen as being too familiar with her: he was in fact tortured into confessing adultery with her.

If the king fancied a good laugh he might summon his fool, Will Somer, to lighten the mood. Will was given licence to poke fun at his master and the courtiers. Pictures show him as rather dour-looking, not in jester's motley but in a plain green livery jacket. His appearance was enlivened by a pink-clothed monkey that sat on his shoulder. Will's patter was to be a country bumpkin, mixing up his words and making earthy comments. It seems however that this was a pose, and that he was an 'artificial fool', or professional comedian. Jane the Fool, retained on the queen's side and later taken into the household of Lady Mary, was a natural fool, a simple-minded girl whose guileless and good-humoured presence would enliven a gathering and take some of the edge off what might be difficult encounters with rival courtiers.

Meanwhile, clearing up after meals was a major task. Washing up was taken to the scullery. The Ordinances laid great stress on the importance of keeping the palace free from all sources of corruption and uncleanness. The master cooks were given an annual allowance to employ scullions, who were not to be such as were accustomed to 'go naked or in garments of such vileness as they now do . . . [nor] lie in the nights and days in the kitchen or ground by the fire-side'. Rather, the new breed of scullions should be apprentices learning to be cooks in their turn, clean and properly clad.

Twice a day, in the morning and afternoon, these scullions, overseen by the sergeant of the hall, would sweep and make clean the 'courts, outward galleries and other places of the court, so as there remain no filth or uncleanness'.

The main sources of rubbish were collected by the servants who kept the courtiers' lodgings. They were ordered not to leave dishes or partially consumed ('broken') meats lying around in the galleries, by their chamber doors or in the courtyards. As soon as they were finished with, the vessels had to be taken down to the squillery. Any food and drink left over had to go to the officers of the almonry 'for the relief of poor folks': it should not be thrown away or given to dogs. The almoner was a cleric of some standing. Wolsey had held the role at the start of his rise to power. As the poor were prevented from clustering round the court, in practice the broken meats would go to an established local charitable foundation, or be sold to catering establishments and the proceeds given to the poor.

8 p.m. To bed

As the bells of the Chapel Royal rang for Compline, the last service of the day, the court prepared for bed.

The meal in the Queen's Chamber and the laughter and merriment that followed were preludes to the king and queen retiring to spend the night together. Although formally their courts and households were so separated that they could have been in different buildings, the fact remains that the king was of an amorous disposition and having children was one of the main purposes of his marriages.

Typically, in the normal course of events, Henry would spend every night or every other night in bed with his wife. This was true even during his short marriage to Anne of Cleves, whom he found physically unattractive. Beside the queen's own bedchamber, there was yet another bedroom, referred to as the King's Chamber on the Queen's Side, which the king and queen used when they were sleeping together.

Although the main entrances to the King's and Queen's Chambers were some distance apart, they were usually so configured that the bedchambers abutted each other. In the original plan of Hampton Court, the Queen's Chambers were immediately above the King's. In the final ground plan, the Queen's Chambers ran along the east side, the King's along the south. They met in the south-east corner.

The configuration of the rooms meant that the king could pass directly to his chamber on the queen's side from his bedchamber on his own side. As only the groom of the stool would accompany the king into these private rooms, and the equivalent chief lady on the queen's side, a reasonable modicum of privacy was afforded to the king and queen. When they emerged into their respective Privy Chambers in the morning, there was no telling exactly where or how they had spent the night. This was doubtless the subject of much discussion by the ladies and gentlemen of their Privy Chambers. Lady Rutland even asked Anne of Cleves outright what had happened in the bedchamber.

The palace did not shut down the moment the king and queen retired for the night. There was still the tidying up and setting up of sleeping arrangements to be done. The gentlemen ushers of the King's and Queen's Chambers would have to make daily records of the bread, ale and wine consumed in the chambers. They would take their records down to the Compting House when they had to fetch 'livery for all night' for the king and queen. This was the food and drink, normally wine and bread, the royal couple might require during the night. It also provided a light breakfast (which was not a formal meal) when they awoke. The gentlemen ushers would place the food on a table or cupboard and attend it until dismissed by one of the gentlemen.

After the king had been 'served for all night', no one was to come into the chambers except the esquires of the body and pages, as well as Privy Chamber staff, who had to take extra care not to disturb the esquires from their rest and sleep. In particular, unless by the king's express permission, there was to be no playing dice or cards in the chamber after the king had gone to bed.

Beds would be made up and all-night livery fetched for the courtiers. It was a mark of King Henry's generous hospitality that beds and beddings were provided for all guests. Staff entitled to would unroll their pallets in the Great Hall. Most of the kitchen staff would bed down on the floors of their freshly cleaned offices, exhausted after their almost continual work.

The pages and esquires of the King's Chamber also slept in their workplaces. Two of the gentlemen of the Privy Chamber were expected every night to sleep on pallets in the King's Privy Chamber. These pallets were prepared by the grooms of the Privy Chamber, who made up the fires and ordered the lights before they departed for their lodgings.

It was a mark of their high favour that other Privy Chamber staff might sleep elsewhere. Henry Norris had his own room next to the King's Closet at Greenwich Palace. His successor as groom of the stool lived in rooms below the Privy Chamber at Hampton Court.

As the gates were closed and all but the essential lights were extinguished, in case of accidental fire, one light was left to burn into the night. In the Compting House, one of the clerks of the green cloth and the chief clerk of comptrollment would be putting the final touches to the daily accounts. These had to be in order before submission to their superiors in the morning. Once the last figure was entered in the final column, they too could turn in for the night, grasping a few short hours of sleep before the sun rose on another day of life in a Tudor palace.